JOHN LOCKE

The Father of Modern Liberalism

Written by Benoît Lefèvre
Translated by Jessica Foster

JOHN LOCKE

KEY INFORMATION

- **Born:** 29 August 1632 in Wrington, Somerset.
- **Died:** 28 October 1704 in Oates, Essex.
- **Context:** The Glorious Revolution and the English Civil War (1642-1689).
- **Main areas of interest:**
    - empiricism
    - social contract theory
    - liberalism
    - the separation of church and state
    - governmental separation of powers.

INTRODUCTION

John Locke was a philosopher and scientist, and is considered to be one of the greatest 17th-century English thinkers. However, his reflections on political philosophy were what he spent most of his time on and owed most of his reputation to.

Drawing inspiration from the works of his predecessors, such as Thomas Hobbes (English philosopher, 1588-1679) and René Descartes (French physicist and philosopher, 1596-1650), Locke developed his thoughts, using empiricism as a starting point. He cultivated a philosophy according to which senses and experience are behind all knowledge of the world. Secondly, human beings can only develop the understanding needed to comprehend complex ideas on the basis of this empiricism.

Additionally, the political and religious turmoil that marked his era and that personally affected him caused him to envisage a new conception of power, exercised by the people and for the people. He also campaigned for the separation of church and state, as well as for religious tolerance. His reflections developed over time, and he published his major works in relatively quick succession: *A Letter Concerning Toleration* and *Two Treatises of Government* were published in 1689, and *An Essay Concerning Human Understanding* was published in 1690. Locke thus developed a philosophy whose influence is only comparable to that of Plato (Greek philosopher, 427-348/7 BC), and which continues to be the basis of our political systems and of liberalism.

BIOGRAPHY

Portrait of John Locke.

A TASTE FOR LEARNING

John Locke was born on 29 August 1632 in Wrington, near Bristol, and spent his childhood nearby. His family were Puritans of the lower nobility. His father was a landowner and a lawyer, and his grandfather was a fabric merchant. Locke had a strict and austere education. In 1647, he entered the prestigious Westminster School in central London, thanks to the influence of Alexander Popham (English politician and Member of Parliament, 1605-1669), under whose command his father had served during the First Civil War (1642-1646). There he learnt ancient languages, including Hebrew, which was reserved for the school's best-performing pupils. However, he did not particularly enjoy it.

In 1652, again with Popham's support, Locke won a scholarship to study at Christ Church, Oxford University, with a view to becoming a minister. However, he disliked the teaching he received there and was more interested in the new sciences: physics, astrophysics and mathematics. But medicine was what interested him the most, and he began to study it keenly. Locke revealed himself to be a true, curious intellectual who would more happily focus on studying than on anything else throughout his life.

In the early 1660s, he also taught at the Church School as a professor of Greek, rhetoric and moral philosophy.

THE BEGINNINGS OF A POLITICAL FIGHT

In the meantime, in 1659 he wrote a letter in which he protested against excessive religious tolerance and criticised Catholics for obeying both the Church and the state. Subsequently, however, he changed his mind during a diplomatic mission to the state of Brandenburg (in modern-day Germany) in late 1665, where he observed that the peaceful coexistence of religions was not only possible, but also beneficial.

In 1666, he met Lord Anthony Ashley Cooper (1621-1683), who was appointed 1st Earl of Shaftesbury in 1672, and became a close friend of his. Locke acted as his personal doctor and political advisor from 1667 onwards. Cooper was strongly opposed to the policies of English King Charles II (1630-1685), for whom he acted as Lord Chancellor. In his opinion, religious persecution was dividing the nation, encouraging emigration and harming trade. Locke was mindful of these ideas and, at his mentor's request, wrote his *Essay Concerning Toleration* (1667), a sort of first draft for his later *Letter Concerning Toleration*. He thus began his reflections on the political and religious issues that were tormenting England and published writings through which he protested against the predominance of religion. He also met several theologians who advocated religious freedom and who would shape his ideas.

FORMATIVE EXPERIENCES ABROAD

Locke spent time in France on two occasions, primarily for health reasons. In fact, he suffered from a lung condition, probably linked to asthma and acute bronchitis. His travels were his opportunity to learn about the philosophical debates that were sweeping the country.

When he returned to England, he went back to Oxford to study philosophy, political science and medicine. A short while later, the king had him watched, as he suspected that Locke's friend Cooper wanted to overthrow him. His fears turned out to be justified: the latter planned a coup with the aim of changing the line of succession to the throne and remove the future King James II (1633-1701). But the plot was eventually discovered and he was sentenced to exile in 1683. Although he could not be blamed for anything, Locke was still afraid of vengeful action and, in 1684, decided to go into preventative exile in the Dutch Republic (modern-day Netherlands). He admired the level of freedom there and discovered the advantages of religious tolerance, which would strongly influence his philosophical reflections. He lived there under a false identity, as James II had recently called for his extradition.

HIS FINAL YEARS

Locke did not return to England until February 1689, once the constitutional monarchy had been established. He became a royal commissioner, in other words a minister, and he was mainly in charge of religious, political and economic affairs. He only held this position for a short amount of time, preferring to fully dedicate himself to his philosophical reflections. However, in 1691, his health started to decline gradually. He then left the political scene and retired to Oates (north-east of London), where he spent the final years of his life. During the summer of 1704, his health worsened considerably. He died in his office on 28 October 1704, and was buried three days later in High Laver, in the graveyard of the parish church.

CONTEXT

ENGLAND IN THE 17TH CENTURY

Before the end of the 17th century, England did not hold the leading position that it would subsequently have on the international scene, although it had produced many famous names, such as William Shakespeare (English playwright, 1564-1616) and Francis Bacon (English statesman and philosopher, 1561-1626). Whether on an economic or an academic level, the continental nations, such as Portugal, Spain, France and, in particular, the Dutch Republic, which was then starting to develop rapidly, were completely overshadowing England. The insular country, however, still saw the development of a scientific elite towards the end of the century. In 1662, the Royal Society, which was aimed at promoting the sciences, was founded. Locke would join it a few years later. In 1676, the Greenwich Observatory was established. In 1682, Edmond Halley (English physicist and astronomer, 1656-1742) studied a comet that had already been observed in 1531 and 1607 and predicted that it would return in 1757 or 1758. Four years later, Isaac Newton (English physicist, astronomer and mathematician, 1642-1727) published his theory of universal gravitation in his work *Philosophiæ Naturalis Principia Mathematica* (1687).

The religious context was also volatile. In England, the head of the Church was not the pope, but the king, after the schism initiated by King Henry VIII (1491-1547). In 1527, the latter had asked the pope to annul his marriage to Catherine of Aragon (1485-1536), as she had not given him a male heir.

When the pope refused, Henry VIII separated from the Catholic Church in 1531 and founded the Anglican Church, of which he declared himself the supreme leader. Religion was subsequently subjected to the rule of the state. While keeping certain elements of Catholicism (the hierarchy of the Church, the recognition of saints, etc.), Henry VIII's successors gradually integrated Protestant practices into Anglicanism (abandoning celibacy for priests and certain sacraments, simplifying access to holy writings, etc.).

THE CREATION OF PARLIAMENT

In the Middle Ages, the feudal relationship between the monarch and his vassal obliged the former to consult the latter for his opinion on various issues, particularly financial matters. It was with this aim that the king summoned his vassals in a consultative assembly. This gradually evolved into Parliament, an institution which became established in the 15th and 16th centuries.

In the early 17th century, King James I (1566-1625) came into conflict with the English Parliament on various matters. James I was both king of England and king of Scotland, and he wanted to unite these two territories into one state, which both the English and Scottish Parliaments categorically refused. But as the absolute monarch of divine right, James I did not accept this resistance.

Portrait of James I.

THE ABSOLUTE MONARCHY OF DIVINE RIGHT

Throughout the Middle Ages and the early modern period, Europe was dominated by absolute monarchs of divine right. This meant that they held complete or almost complete power over their subjects. At that time, two types of power coexisted: spiritual power, which was in the hands of religious leaders, and temporal power, embodied by sovereigns. The latter was legitimate, as he followed the will of God, which also conferred a sort of spiritual power onto monarchs.

At the same time, James I concluded a peace agreement with Spain, against whom piracy had been committed and authorised. The pillaging of Spanish ships that traded with colonies was a significant source of revenue at that time. This is why Parliament disliked the decision so intensely and refused to give their approval, which was necessary for levying taxes.

These tensions did not diminish during the reign of his successor, Charles I (1600-1649). In fact, in 1629, he decided to levy another tax without consulting Parliament. The events that followed led to civil war in the 1640s. This saw the opposition of the Royalists, who advocated for a high concentration of power in the hands of the king, and Parliamentarians, led by Oliver Cromwell (1599-1658), who were in favour of a reduction of the monarchy's power in favour of a Parliament that represented the people.

In 1649, the English Parliament decided to launch an impeachment procedure against Charles I, which in principle involved trying the king's close collaborators. Its application to the monarch provoked strong reactions in Europe, where the absolute monarchy of divine right was prevalent, as it seemed to rebel against God's will.

But this had no effect, and the process was launched. After Charles I's execution, on 30 January 1649, Oliver Cromwell, the self-declared Lord Protector of the Commonwealth, abolished the monarchy, established a republic and implemented a written constitution in 1653. His time in power saw the rise of extremely authoritarian politics that were particularly intolerant towards Catholics. Cromwell reigned as a sovereign and even went as far as to designate his son as his successor. Parliament had had enough, withdrew their support for Cromwell's Protectorate and re-established the monarchy in 1660, recalling the legitimate heir to the throne, Charles II.

DID YOU KNOW?

Nowadays, unlike most other Western countries, the United Kingdom does not have a written constitution. This would only serve as a reminder of Cromwell's authoritarianism and, moreover, proves that such a document is no guarantee against absolutism. The country does, nonetheless, have a long tradition of important texts that set out royal powers and guarantee the rights of the people, such as the Magna Carta (1215), the Petition of Right (1628) and the Habeas Corpus Act (1679).

Despite the reestablishment of the monarchy, tensions subsisted. The royal family was still bitter towards Parliament, which they held responsible for the death of James I, and towards Anglicans, who had persecuted Catholics.

THE FIRST STEPS OF PARLIAMENTARY DEMOCRACY

Once again, Parliament emerged victorious following tensions with royalty. Indeed, at the end of the Glorious Revolution (1688-1689), it enacted the Bill of Rights, which aimed to force the abdication of James II, who had succeeded his brother Charles II, in favour of his daughter, Mary II (1662-1694). She was trusted by Parliament, as she was married to a Protestant, William of Orange (1650-1702), who, moreover, had the support of John Locke. When this text was signed in February 1689, they came to the throne. The Bill of Rights was fundamentally important, and set out the principles of establishing a new regime, parliamentary democracy, which gave the people certain fundamental rights, limited royal power and demanded Parliament's consent for the king to levy taxes. It resembled an actual contract between the monarchy and Parliament, which represented the people it had been elected by. It was also undoubtedly inspired by the ideas put forward by Locke in his *Two Treatises of Government*.

18th-century engraving of the Bill of Rights being presented to William and Mary.

This long period of turmoil that England experienced during the 17th century was conducive to the development of political reflections. In fact, many thinkers tried to develop theories in order to implement a new form of power in which the people would no longer be subject to the absolutism of a king who considered his legitimacy to be the result of divine will. Hobbes was a good example of this. In 1651, he wrote *Leviathan*, in which he compared the monarchy to a biblical creature with several heads that could only survive if one of them took decisions. The king embodied this thinking head, which drew its legitimacy not from God, but from the submission of the powers of others. According to Hobbes, this delegation was final and irreversible. Thus, even if the king was conducting himself badly in politics, he could not be overthrown. Locke would subsequently attempt to define the limits of this absolute power described by his predecessor.

LOCKE'S POLITICAL THEORIES

A *TABULA RASA* AS A STARTING POINT

Locke established a principle according to which the human mind resembles a blank slate, devoid of any preconceived ideas. This *tabula rasa* gradually fills due to experience, which itself comes from two sources: it is either perceived by the senses or conceived by reflection, and therefore by the human mind.

Starting from this principle, Locke attempted to devise a new political system that would put the people first. Thus, much like Hobbes, he established a theory founded on the succession of two distinct states in society.

THE STATE OF NATURE AND THE CIVIL STATE

Locke was inspired by Dutch theories, particularly those of Hugo Grotius (1583-1645), which he had studied during his exile to the Dutch Republic during the 1680s. Locke believed that humans began life in a state of nature, in other words a community that was not yet organised by a political power. They lived in a state of freedom, equality, value and rights, which God had given to them, along with everything on Earth. For Hobbes, this led to a total absence of rules and to a permanent state of war in which everyone tried to protect their lives at the expense of other people's lives. On the contrary, Locke agreed with a theory developed by Grotius stating that a natural law was imposed on humans, and that this constituted the only limit to their existence.

Portrait of Hugo Grotius, dated 1631.

The right to property, in a broad sense, constituted the essential element of this natural right. It must apply to everyone, without any distinction. Everyone is the individual owner of their body and anything that ensures their survival, in other words, what they obtain through work. People therefore have the right to protect their existence, freedom and personal possessions, as long as they respect the lives of others. However, this last point is where the difficulty lies. Everyone can punish those that harm them, and thus violate this natural law, although this is still somewhat problematic. In fact, due to the pride that exists within everyone, men can be biased, always acting for their own benefit or for that of those close to them. There is therefore serious insecurity in this state of nature, as there is no way of impartially judging the non-respect of individual rights.

PROPERTY

The term 'property' comes from the Latin 'proprietas', meaning something that has a specific individual characteristic. Locke understood the notion of property in a very broad sense. Thus, according to the English philosopher, humans were the owners of their own person and their own life, and could also be the owner of any other objects. In fact, man drew his identity and specific character from what he owned, in other words his conscience, his physical sensations, his ideas, his memory, etc.

To mitigate this insecurity, individuals implicitly choose to agree on a social contract to form a society for themselves and move to a civil state. This pact must be agreed upon freely; nothing can be forced to leave the state of nature. By approving it, everyone renounces their prerogatives in some way to delegate them to a civil authority, considered to be more impartial and more effective. In order to do this, all the individuals who make up this political community implement a political power, tasked with defending property and people's various rights, through elections. Its representatives are tasked with, on the one hand, establishing laws to protect individuals and, on the other hand, using the necessary force to punish those who pose a threat to society by breaking the rules. The penalties resulting from this can extend as far as death. The idea is that decisions made by representatives are those shared by private persons, as they are meant to act in their interests.

Thus, at this time, Parliament held legislative power, while executive power was still in the hands of the monarch. Locke was innovative on this point by laying the foundations of the idea of the separation of powers. However, as the only source of political power, the people had a right to resistance which they could use if the government began to abuse the power that had been conferred on it. The people could thus overthrow the government by force and establish a new regime. In practice, in England at the time, this right to resistance could be applied:

- if the king used arbitrary power to the detriment of the laws;
- if he prevented the legislative assembly from using its power freely;
- if he blocked the people from electing one or more representatives;
- if the king or Parliament placed the people under the domination of a foreign power;
- if one of the two powers acted without respecting its role

to protect the property of individuals;
- if the executive turned out to be incapable of enforcing laws.

Consequently, Locke dared to grant legitimacy to a sort of rebellion, according to very precise circumstances. In this way, he stood out from his predecessors, who had always shown distrust towards anything that might destabilise the social order. Even Voltaire (1694-1778) and Jean-Jacques Rousseau (1712-1778), whom Locke greatly influenced, would not have this audacity.

PROPERTY AND THE CAPITALISATION OF GOODS

As we have seen, property constituted a fundamental element of Locke's philosophy. Humans gained possessions through work. As a result, private property supplanted collective property. This was especially true in view of the fact that, of the goods used, those that came directly from nature had a miniscule share compared to those produced by man. It was therefore work that created most wealth, which itself belonged to private owners. This appropriation of goods was still legitimate if the surpluses were then re-distributed, in one way or another, to a third party, in order to help them to satisfy their needs. But Locke believed that it was normal for a rich man to gain compensation from giving the fruits of his labour to someone else, hence the point of an exchange.

This is how Locke justified the necessity of money, an object that is, in itself, completely useless, unlike clothes or food. Unlike food, it is not perishable, and therefore people can keep it for as long as they want without it deteriorating in some way. They can even accumulate more of it than necessary. In addition, some people do not think twice before acquiring a disproportionate amount of it, creating stark inequalities between individuals. With this theory, Locke briefly summarised the history of capitalism. This theory would later be developed more fully by Thomas Robert Malthus (British economist, 1766-1834) the following century.

Moreover, in Locke's time, the Earth was thought to be large enough for everyone to have a plot of land and cultivate it to feed themselves. If needs be, therefore, moving would be sufficient. This sentiment was reinforced by the colonisation of North America, which had an enormous amount of as of yet unexploited land. Locke, however, turned this idea of eternal abundance on its head, noticing the gradual growth of the population and the progress being made by industry, which was leading to greater and greater needs.

THE *LETTER CONCERNING TOLERATION* AND THE SEPARATION OF CHURCH AND STATE

A

LETTER

CONCERNING

Toleration :

Humbly Submitted, &c.

—————

LICENSED, *Octob.* 3. 1689.

—————

LONDON,

Printed for *Awnsham Churchill*, at the *Black Swan* at *Amen-Corner*. 1689.

Title page of the first edition of Locke's *Letter Concerning Toleration*.

Drawing on his *Essay Concerning Toleration*, which he had

written in 1667, Locke wrote the *Letter Concerning Toleration* (1689), which would become a point of reference on the matter of the separation of church and state. It was no accident that he began writing this work in 1685, during his exile in the Dutch Republic. The same year, Louis XIV (1638-1715) revoked the Edict of Nantes, which had previously authorised Protestants to practice their religion in France. Unless they renounced their religion, they were forced into exile, and many of them moved to the Dutch Republic. The matter of religious intolerance also affected England, as James II, who was a devout Catholic, also persecuted Protestants. Locke felt particularly affected by this issue.

Inspired by the Dutch Jewish philosopher Spinoza (1632-1677), among others, Locke developed a theory that proposed separating the church and the state. He defended each individual's freedom to publicly practice their religion as, in his opinion, the state could not intervene in people's faith. Its role had to be restricted to protecting rights and imposing penalties on those who broke the law. The Church was responsible for the salvation of souls and could therefore threaten lawbreakers with sentences that would take effect after death, but not during earthly life; at worst, it could excommunicate an individual from their religious community. True faith, Locke emphasised, was something much too private and personal to be changed by force or punishment.

THE *TWO TREATISES OF GOVERNMENT* AND THE DISTINCTION OF POWERS

In 1689, Locke anonymously published his major work, *Two Treatises of Government*, in which he presented his reflections on the rights of individuals, their freedom, their property, and rebellion. The first part aimed to deconstruct the principles of hereditary monarchy of divine right. This text was the answer to *Patriarcha*, the posthumous work of Robert Filmer (English philosopher, 1588-1653), published in 1680, which defended absolutism and stated that monarchs were the successors of Adam and their divine right originated in Biblical texts.

In the second part, Locke analysed the basis of the legitimacy of government power. He believed that humans did not obey a man or a group, but laws. These laws could not be random and had to guarantee both the common good and individual freedom. Including the idea of the separation of powers, he therefore saw legislative power as the supreme power. Executive power, on the other hand, was responsible for establishing the means by which to apply these laws. Locke identified a third and final power, federal power, which concerned external relations and foreign affairs.

According to Locke, the government could only be legitimate if it respected the distinction between these three powers.

THE *ESSAY CONCERNING HUMAN UNDERSTANDING* AND THE BIRTH OF IDEAS

In 1690, Locke published his *Essay Concerning Human Understanding*, in which he tried to develop a theory that justified religious and philosophical tolerance.

Locke was opposed to all dogmatic thought and was convinced that certainties were as rare as they were limited. This is what he tried to prove in his essay. Firstly, he explained that understanding, or the part of the human mind that allows people to understand the world around them, transforms the different information the mind receives into ideas. It then establishes certainties based on this information. It is important to be aware of the fact that mistakes could happen, given that human understanding is based on perceptions. Hence it is necessary to make a distinction between the real nature of things – what they are – as in their qualities, and their appearance – the way in which they are perceived, the idea the individual gets of them – as in the general sense. This is a fundamental principle at the basis of modern philosophy.

Locke also dealt with the matter of self-awareness. He reconsidered the principle of *cogito ergo sum* ("I think therefore I am"), developed by Descartes, according to which having thoughts and being aware of them is proof of existence. But Locke went further with this reflection. In fact, according to the English philosopher, an individual does not think all the time and is consequently not always aware. This means that an individual can only be held responsible for the actions they commit in full awareness. By way of this demonstration, Locke defined human beings in terms of individuality and not in relation to a group. This is why he is considered to be the father of modern individualism, which is not satisfied with defining man as part of a social group, even if the idea of the subconscious, which would be found later on in the work of Leibniz (1646-1716) and Sigmund Freud (1856-1939), was a concept that was never particularly developed in his philosophy.

In this work, Locke also tried to deconstruct innatism, a theory close to Descartes' heart according to which certain ideas are not acquired, but are ingrained in the human mind as they are present from birth. In Locke's view, knowledge is mainly acquired through the individual's experience in the world around them. In his reflection, he went as far as to wonder about the innatism of the existence of God. To do this, he reconsidered one of Descartes' theories, according to which human ideas come from God, who acts as a point of reference.

Portrait of René Descartes.

This work was extremely successful in Europe, particularly after it was translated into French in 1700 by Pierre Coste (1668-1747), a Protestant in exile in London, and thanks to Voltaire, who drew inspiration from it when writing his analysis of the mind in his *Letters on the English* (1734).

IMPACT

EMPIRICISM VS. ESSENTIALISM

In Locke's era, there were two opposing schools of thought regarding ways of understanding the world. The empiricist method, which Locke developed, involved observing specific cases with a view to subsequently coming up with generalisations. Although it was praised and adopted by many philosophers, this philosophy was also harshly criticised by others, who opted for an opposite and more traditional approach, based on the essence of things, meaning the elements that made things what they were. In this case, hypotheses were then formulated to explain the causes of various phenomena. This is what Descartes did.

Leibniz carefully studied the *Essay Concerning Human Understanding* and tried to communicate with Locke, but in vain. He then began to write his *New Essays on Human Understanding* in 1703, but it would not be published until 1765, long after the death of both of the thinkers. It was a fictional dialogue between the two philosophers, who confronted each other with their respective theories, as Leibniz supported an essentialist approach to understanding, contrary to Locke.

ECONOMIC LIBERALISM

Nowadays, we often think of liberalism as an economic concept, but Locke gave it a much broader definition. In fact, by liberalism, he meant the desire to protect the individual rights and freedoms of the population. The reason that this definition is no longer really used now is due in particular to the Scottish philosopher and economist Adam Smith (1723-1790), who elaborated the economic aspects of Locke's principle of liberalism. According to Smith, society exists thanks to an economic link. Men are united not by a common desire to protect individual rights and freedoms as Locke understood them, but by the exchange of goods that they need. Society is therefore governed by natural economic laws: supply and demand. This economic market has to run itself. The state can only intervene to guarantee private ownership of the means of production, freedom of work, competition and free trade.

LOCKE'S INFLUENCE IN THE UNITED STATES

The separation of powers devised by Locke is at the basis of the constitutions of various modern democracies, particularly that of the United States. He had an undeniable influence on the early years of the country's independence: several writers of the Declaration of Independence (4 July 1776), including Thomas Jefferson (1743-1826), were admirers of the English philosopher.

Moreover, the second article of the Declaration of Independence draws on some of Locke's principles:

- equality between men, who have natural inalienable rights linked to the protection of their lives;
- the agreement of the people in establishing a government responsible for guaranteeing these rights;

- the right to resistance.

Additionally, it was the last point that legitimised America's independence. In fact, in 1773, the 13 American colonies that belonged to England at the time broke with the English Parliament, in an event known as the Boston Tea Party, as they believed that they were wronged by its policies.

The American Constitution was complemented in 1789 by the American Bill of Rights, which guaranteed individual rights and freedoms, notably in terms of property.

THE ENLIGHTENMENT

Locke's ideas heavily influenced French Enlightenment philosophers. His empiricist philosophy, considered a model of wisdom, was popular among the intellectuals of his time, much more so than the metaphysics of Descartes and Leibniz. Rousseau adopted his visions of freedom and equality in the state of nature in his work *The Social Contract* in 1762. Montesquieu (1689-1755) was also influenced by the English philosopher and, in 1748, adopted the principles of the separation of powers in his work *The Spirit of the Laws*. In the same way as Locke had done, he distinguished between legislative and executive powers, as well as judicial power – no longer federal power. This conception of the three powers can be seen today in all modern democracies.

In 1789, the French revolutionaries were also inspired to a considerable extent by Locke's ideas in the Declaration of the Rights of Man and of the Citizen. They aligned themselves with Rousseau, who had indisputably been influenced by the English philosopher. The first two articles thus recall the principles of natural law that had been proposed a century earlier by Locke:

> "Men are born and remain free and equal in rights. Social distinctions may be founded only upon the general good." (Article 1)
> "The aim of all political association is the preservation of the natural and imprescriptible rights of man. These rights are liberty, property, security, and resistance to oppression." (Article 2)

The third article reminds us that "[t]he principle of all sovereignty resides essentially in the nation", which recalls Locke's civil community. As for the law, it must be "the expression of the general will", and "[e]very citizen has a right to participate personally, or through his representative, in its foundation" (Article 6). The rest of the Declaration essentially elaborates on Locke's ideas, by defining the limits of power, particularly legislative power, in order to prevent any form of authoritarianism. This clearly shows that this resolutely modern philosopher was highly significant.

Declaration of the Rights of Man and of the Citizen, painting by Jean-Jacques-François Le Barbier.

SUMMARY

- All of Locke's philosophical reflections are based on empiricism. He believed that human experience is responsible for knowledge.
- Locke was heavily influenced by his times. He developed his philosophical theories to respond to the problems that had arisen in Europe at the time, particularly in England.
- To find answers to his questions, he drew on his own experience and on the many encounters he had throughout his life, especially abroad, where he discovered the benefits of religious tolerance.
- Locke was part of a double intellectual movement that was very active in the early 17th century. On the one hand, he was part of a political and scientific wave that would bring England to the forefront of the international scene. On the other hand, he was contributing to a wider European philosophical trend that was responding to the problems of the era, and was looking for a new political system that would separate religion from the state, thus placing the people at the centre of power.
- He had also long been interested in the notion of freedom, which he did not see as an absolute right. Rather, he believed that people should not be subjected to the arbitrary power of others, making this notion not a power, but a social relationship. It was therefore the supremacy of the law that made freedom possible, but it had to rid itself of any ambiguity. This is why it had to be clear, general (as in universal, and not the result of

anyone's arbitrary decision), non-retroactive, stable, public (everyone had to be able to find out about it) and fair.

- Locke also developed a vision of capitalism. He was one of the first thinkers to realise that the planet's resources were limited in the face of economic development.
- Locke had a considerable impact on our modern society. In fact, his conception of the separation of powers is at the basis of all modern democracies. Additionally, his thoughts influenced many later philosophers, such as Voltaire, Rousseau and Leibniz.

We want to hear from you!
Leave a comment on your online library
and share your favourite books on social media!

FIND OUT MORE

BIBLIOGRAPHY

- De Brabandere, L. and Deprez, S. (2007) John Locke. *La Libre Belgique*, 18 December 2007, p. 27.
- Brykman, G. (2008) Locke (John). *Encyclopædia Universalis: Corpus*, vol. 14. Paris: Encyclopædia Universalis, pp. 632-635.
- Cottret, B. (2003) *Histoire d'Angleterre XVIe-XVIIe siècle*. Paris: PUF.
- Lazzeri, C. (2007) Locke (1632-1704) : bonheur et obligation morale. *Histoire raisonnée de la philosophie morale et politique*, vol. 1. Paris: Flammarion, pp. 431-446.
- Le Point (2012) Les maîtres de la raison : les textes fondamentaux. *Références*, n° 41, September-October 2012.
- Marx, R. and Chassaigne, P. (2004) *Histoire de la Grande-Bretagne*. Paris: Perrin.
- Milton, J. R. (2004) John Locke. *Oxford Dictionary of National Biography*, vol. 34. New York: Oxford University Press, pp. 216-228.
- Morfaux, L.-M. and Lefranc, J. (2007) *Nouveau vocabulaire de la philosophie et des sciences humaines*. Paris: Armand Colin.
- Nemo, P. (2013) *Histoire des idées politiques aux Temps modernes et contemporains*. Paris: PUF.
- Nuovo, V. (no date) Locke, John. *Encyclopedia of the Enlightenment*, vol. 2. Oxford: Oxford University Press, pp. 427-431.
- Renaut, A. (1999) *Histoire de la philosophie politique*.

Paris: Calmann-Lévy.

- Tremolieres, F. (no date) Essai sur l'entendement humain. Livre de John Locke. *Universalis.fr.* [Online]. [Accessed 22 August 2015]. Available from: <http://www.universalis.fr/encyclopedie/essai-sur-l-entendement-humain/>

ICONOGRAPHIC SOURCES

- Portrait of John Locke. Royalty-free reproduction picture.
- Portrait of James I. Royalty-free reproduction picture.
- 18th-century engraving of the Bill of Rights being presented to William and Mary. Royalty-free reproduction picture.
- Portrait of Hugo Grotius, dated 1631. Royalty-free reproduction picture.
- Title page of the first edition of Locke's *Letter Concerning Toleration*. Royalty-free reproduction picture.
- Portrait of René Descartes. Royalty-free reproduction picture. Royalty-free reproduction picture.
- *Declaration of the Rights of Man and of the Citizen,* painting by Jean-Jacques-François Le Barbier. Royalty-free reproduction picture.

www.50minutes.com

Ebook EAN: 9782806296733

Paperback EAN: 9782806296740

Legal Deposit: D/2017/12603/229

Cover: © Primento

Digital conception by Primento, the digital partner of publishers.